Symphony No. 2
in C Minor
("Resurrection")

Gustav Mahler

DOVER PUBLICATIONS, INC.
Mineola, New York

Bibliographical Note

This Dover edition, first published in 1997, is a republication of *Zweite Symphonie in C Moll,* originally published by Josef Weinberger, Vienna; copyright 1897 by Friedrich Hofmeister, Leipzig. Lists of contents and instrumentation are newly added. The English translations of the vocal texts were prepared specially for this edition.

International Standard Book Number: 0-486-29952-X

Manufactured in the United States of America
Dover Publications, Inc., 31 East 2nd Street, Mineola, N.Y. 11501

CONTENTS

Symphony No. 2
in C Minor
("Resurrection")
(1888–94 / revised orchestration, 1903)

TEXTS AND TRANSLATIONS

URLICHT (Primal Light) is a poem from *Des Knaben Wunderhorn*—"The Youth's Magic Horn"— an 1805 anthology of German folk poetry gathered by poet Clemens Brentano and antiquarian Achim von Arnim. It is set for alto solo in movement 4, page 126. AUFERSTEH'N (Resurrection), a poem by Friedrich Gottlieb Klopstock, is set for soprano solo and chorus in movement 5, page 184. O GLAUBE, MEIN HERZ (O believe, my heart) is Mahler's own text. It is set for alto and soprano soli and chorus in movement 5, page 191.

URLICHT

O Röschen roth!
Der Mensch liegt in größter Noth!
Der Mensch liegt in größter Pein!
Je lieber möcht' ich in Himmel sein!
Da kam ich auf einen breiten Weg;
Da kam ein Engelein und wollt' mich abweisen.
Ach nein! Ich ließ mich nicht abweisen:
Ich bin von Gott und will wieder zu Gott!
Der liebe Gott wird mir ein Lichtchen geben,
Wird leuchten mir bis in das ewig selig Leben!

PRIMAL LIGHT

O little red rose!
Man lies in the greatest need.
Man lies in the greatest suffering.
How much rather would I be in Heaven!
I came upon a broad road.
There came an angel and wanted to block my way.
Ah no! I did not let myself be turned away!
I am of God, and to God I shall return.
Dear God will grant me a small light,
Will light my way to eternal, blissful life.

AUFERSTEH'N

Aufersteh'n, ja aufersteh'n wirst du,
Mein Staub, nach kurzer Ruh!
Unsterblich Leben
Wird der dich rief dir geben.

Wieder aufzublüh'n wirst du gesät!
Der Herr der Ernte geht
Und sammelt Garben
Uns ein, die starben.

RESURRECTION

Arise, yes, you will arise from the dead,
My dust, after a short rest!
Eternal life
Will be given you by Him who called you.

To bloom again are you sown.
The lord of the harvest goes
And gathers the sheaves,
Us who have died.

O GLAUBE, MEIN HERZ

O glaube, mein Herz, o glaube:
Es geht dir nichts verloren!

Dein ist, was du gesehnt!
Dein, was du geliebt, was du gestritten!

O glaube:
Du wardst nicht umsonst geboren!
Hast nicht umsonst gelebt, gelitten!

Was entstanden ist, das muß vergehen!
Was vergangen, auferstehen!
Hör' auf zu beben!
Bereite dich zu leben!

O Schmerz! Du Alldurchdringer!
Dir bin ich entrungen!
O Tod! Du Allbezwinger!
Nun bist du bezwungen!
Mit Flügeln, die ich mir errungen
In heißem Liebesstreben
Werd' ich entschweben
Zum Licht, zu dem kein Aug' gedrungen!
Sterben werd' ich, um zu leben!

Auferstehn, ja auferstehn wirst du,
Mein Herz, in einem Nu!
Was du geschlagen,
Zu Gott wird es dich tragen!

O BELIEVE, MY HEART

Oh believe, my heart, oh believe,
Nothing will be lost to you!

Everything is yours that you have desired,
Yours, what you have loved,
*   what you have struggled for!*

Oh believe,
You were not born in vain,
Have not lived in vain, suffered in vain!

What was created must perish!
What has perished must rise again!
Tremble no more!
Prepare yourself to live!

O Sorrow, all-penetrating!
I have been wrested away from you!
O Death, all-conquering!
Now you are conquered!
With wings that I won
In the passionate strivings of love
I shall mount
To the light to which no sight has penetrated.
I shall die, so as to live!

Arise, yes, you will arise from the dead,
My heart, in an instant!
What you have conquered
Will bear you to God.

INSTRUMENTATION

WINDS

4 Flutes [Flöte, Fl.]
Flutes double 4 Piccolos

4 Oboes [Oboe, Ob.]
Oboes 3, 4 double English Horns [Engl. Horn]

3 Clarinets in C, A, Bb("B") [Clarinette, Clar.]
Clarinet 3 doubles Bass Clarinet in Bb ("B") [Bass-Clarinette, Basscl.]

2 Clarinets in Eb [Clarinette (Es)]
Clarinet 2 doubles a 4th Bb Clarinet

3 Bassoons [Fagott, Fag.]
Bassoon 3 doubles Contrabassoon [Contra-Fagott, Contrafg.]

BRASS

10 Horns in F [Horn]
4 horns offstage ["in der Ferne"]

8–10 Trumpets in C, F [Trompete, Trmp.]
4-to-6 trumpets offstage

4 Trombones [Posaune, Pos.]

Contrabass-Tuba [Contrabasstuba, Tuba]

STRINGS *(largest possible contingent)*

Violins I, II [Violine, Viol.]
Violas [Viola]
Cellos [Violoncello, Cello]
Basses [Contrabass, Bass]
(Several with low C-string)

PERCUSSION *(7 players)*

7 Timpani [Pauken]
6 instruments (3 players) onstage; one instrument offstage

2 Pairs of Cymbals [Becken]
One pair offstage

2 Triangles [Triangel]
One offstage

Side Drum [Kleine Trommel, Kl. Tr.]
More than one if possible

Glockenspiel

3 Bells [Glocken]
Steel rods with deep, unpitched sound

2 Bass Drums [Grosse Trommel, Gr. Tr.]
One offstage, with switch* [Ruthe]

2 Tam-tams
One high, one low

HARP [Harfe]

ORGAN [Orgel]

VOICES

Soprano solo [Sopr(an)-Solo]
Alto solo [Altstimme, Altst., Alt. Solo]
Full Chorus
   Sopranos [Sopr(ane)]
   Altos [Alt(e)]
   Tenors [Ten(ore)]
   Basses [Bässe, Bass]

---

* "Some composers have indicated the use of a switch for a rough, slappy sound."
(Smith Brindle, *Contemporary Percussion.* Oxford University Press, 1970.)

Symphony No. 2
in C Minor
("Resurrection")

1

Allegro maestoso. Mit durchaus ernstem und feierlichem Ausdruck.

1. 2. Flöte.

3. Flöte (Piccolo) (im *ff* doppelt besetzt)

1. 2. Oboe.

3. Oboe (engl. Horn.)   Engl. Horn.

1. 2. 3. Clarinette in B.
(3. nimmt zuweilen Bassclar. in B.)

1. 2. Clarinette in Es.

1. 2. Fagott.   zu 2

3. Fagott (Contrafagott.)   Contrafagott

6 Hörner in F.
(Die Bezeichnung „gestopft" gilt, bis sie durch
eine neue „offen" wieder aufgehoben ist.)

4 Trompeten in F.
(1. Tromp. im *ff* doppelt besetzt.)

4 Posaunen.
(mit Sordinen versehen)

Contrabasstuba.

Triangel. Tam-tam.(tief)

Becken (abwechselnd mit einem Tam-
tam. welches höher klingt als das 1. und
mit Tam-tam (hoch) bezeichnet ist.)

Grosse Trommel.

1. 2. Pauke.

1. 2. Harfe.

Allegro maestoso. Mit durchaus ernstem und feierlichem Ausdruck.

1. Violine.   trem. (nicht theilen.)
ff   *p*

2. Violine   trem. (nicht theilen.)
ff   *p*

Viola.   trem. (getheilt.)
ff   *p*

Violoncell.   accel.
wild *fff*   accel.

Contrabass.
mindestens einige davon mit Contra-C-Saite   wild *fff*

Allegro maestoso. Mit durchaus ernstem und feierlichem Ausdruck.

Anmerkung für den Dirigenten. In den ersten Takten des Thema's sind die Bassfiguren schnell in heftigem Ansturm ungefähr ♩=144. die Pausen jedoch im Hauptzeitmass
♩=84-92 auszuführen. Der Halt im 4. Takte ist kurz — gleichsam ein Ausholen zu neuer Kraft.

*) untere Stimme nur von den mit Contra-C versehenen Bässen auszuführen.

6

59
zu 2
1. 2. Picc.
1. 2. Fl.
1. 2. Ob.
1. 2. Fag.
1. 2. Horn in F.
3. 4. Horn in F.
5. 6.
1. 2. Pos.
1. Pauke 2.
1. Viol.
2. Viol.
Viola
Cello u. Bass unis.
molto cresc.
1. nimmt Flöte
Wie zu Anfang.
Vorwärts.
Più mosso subito.
cresc.
gest.
mit Sord.
Sordinen ab!
B nach C.
nicht theilen
theilen
dim.
4
67
a tempo (poco più mosso)
zu 3
1. 2. 3. Fl.
1. 2. 3. Ob.
1. 2. Clar. in B.
1. 2. Fag.
Contrafg.
1. 3. Horn in F.
2. 4. Horn in F.
5. 6.
offen
geth.
sempre p

10

16

179
11
Tempo I.
1. 2.
Fl.
3.
zu 2.
1. 2.
Ob.
3.
1.
Clar. in B.
2. 3.
1. 2. Fag.
Contrafag.
Tempo I.
1. 2.
Horn in F.
3. 4.
Horn in F.
5. 6.
zu 2.
2. 4. Trmp. in F.
1. 2. Pos.
4. Pos. u. Tuba.
1.
Pauke
2.
sempre p
Cis nach D.
Tempo I.
geth.
1. Viol.
2. Viol.
G-Saite
Viola.
Cello.
Bass.
11
Tempo I.

21

*) Falls die Bässe keine C-Saite haben,
sind 2 derselben herunter zu stim-
men, die Uebrigen pausiren.

28

Von hier an <u>unmerklich</u> allmählich in ein etwas strafferes Tempo übergehen.

Hier ist das Zeitmaass durch die vorangegangene unmerkliche Steigerung
bereits „**Energisch bewegt**" (ohne zu eilen) geworden; dasselbe ist noch
immer weiter zu steigern bis zum Eintritt des **a tempo** (Più mosso.)

289
Anmerkung für den Dirigenten: „CÄSUR" und hierauf plötzlich vorwärts!
Molto riten.
18
a tempo subito.
Molto più mosso.
1.2. Piccolo.
1.2. Fl.
1.2.3. Ob.
1.2. Clar in B.
1. Es Clar. 2.
1.2. Fag.
Contrafag.
1.2. Horn in F.
3.4. Horn in F.
5.6.
1.2. Trmp. in F.
3.4.
1.2. Pos.
3. Pos.
4.
Tuba.
Triangel.
Becken.
1 Pauke. 2
1. Viol.
2. Viol.
Viola.
Cello.
Bass.
zu 2.
zu 3.
molto rit.
ff a tempo (Molto più mosso)
Schalltrichter auf.
cresc.
mit Dämpfer
mit Teller
Holzschlägel!
sempre ff
dim.
geth.

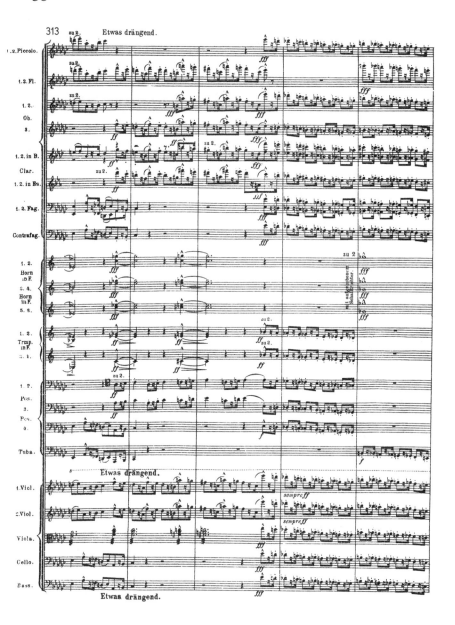

325
20 Molto pesante.
1.2. Piccolo.
1.2. Fl.
1.2 Ob. 3.
1.2. Clar. in B. 3.
1.2. Fag.
Contrafag.
1.3. Horn in F.
5.2. Horn in F. 4.6.
1.2. Trmp. in F. 3.4.
1.2. Pos. 3.4.
Tuba.
Becken.
Gr. Tr.
1. Pauke. 2.
Molto pesante.
1. Viol.
2. Viol.
Viola.
Cello.
Bass.
20 Molto pesante.
zu 2.
offen
mit Holzschlägel
sempre ff
mit Schwammschlägel
arco
pizz.
Rit.
molto cresc.
Tempo I.
geth.

350
22
1.-2. Fl.
3.
1. 2. Ob.
engl. Horn
1. 2. in B. Clar.
3. in C.
1. 2. Fag.
Contrafag.
1. 2. Horn in F.
3. 4. Horn in F.
5. 6.
1. 2. Trmp. in F.
3. 4.
1. 2. Pos.
3. 4.
Tuba
1. Viol.
2. Viol.
Viola
Cello
Bass
zu 2.
22

50

52

Hier folgt eine Pause von mindestens 5 Minuten.

Nicht eilen. Sehr gemächlich.

58

3

78

88

221
1.2.Piccolo.
1.2. Fl.
1.2. Ob. 3.
2.3. in B. Clar. 1.2. in Es.
1.2. Fag.
Contrafg.
1.2. Horn in F.
3.4. Horn in F.
5.6.
1.2. Trmp. in F. 3.4.
Triangel.
Becken.
1. Pauke.
1. Viol.
2. Viol.
Viola.
Cello.
Bass.
zu 2
zu 3
nicht getheilt

39
257
1.2.Piccolo.
1.2.Fl.
1.2.3.Ob.
1.2.3.in C.
Clar.
1.2.in Es.
1.2.Fag.
Contrafg.
1.3.5.
Horn
in F.
2.4.6.
1.
Trmp.
in F.
2.
Trmp.
in F.
3.4.
Triangel.
Becken.
1.
Pauke
2.
1.Viol.
2.Viol.
Viola.
Celli.
Bass.
zu 2
zu 3
ff
fp
f
p
tr
nicht getheilt
39

98

110

114

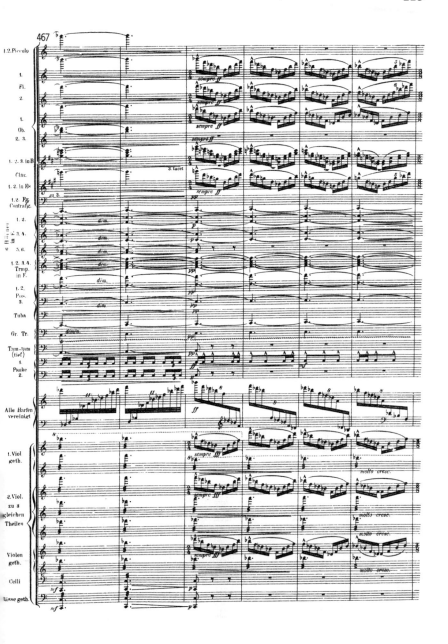

116

120

124

Folgt ohne jede Unterbrechung der 4. Satz.

attacca: 4
"URLICHT"
(from *Des Knaben Wunderhorn*)

132

*) Wenn nicht wenigstens ein Bassist das Contra C auf seinem Instrument zur Verfügung hat, so spielen sämmtliche Bassisten unisono die Oberstimme.
+) Anmerk. f. d. Dirigenten: hier, wie bei der folgende gleichartigen Stelle ist darauf zu achten, dass sich die Triller der 1. u 2. Geigen dicht an einander schliessen

und keine Pause dazwischen entsteht (eine „Trillerkette") also so:

Die mit △ bezeichneten Noten länger gehalten.

145

176
1.2. Fl.
1.2.
Ob.
3.4.
1.2. in B.
Clar.
1.2. in Es.
1.2.
Fag.
3.
Contrafag.
1.3.
Horn
in F.
2.4.
Horn
in F.
5.6.
1.2.
Trmp.
in F.
3.4.
Trmp.
in F.
5.6.
1.2.
Pos.
3.4.
Tuba
1.
Pauke
2.
Harfen
1. Viol.
2. Viol.
Viola
Cello
Bass
zu 2
zu 2.
sempre ff

*) Wenn nicht mindestens 2 Contrabässe das „Contra C" besitzten, so wird von allen Bässen blos die Oberstimme dieser 5 Takte gespielt.

*) sehr langsam und stetig bis zur höchsten Kraft anschwellend.

158

277
Immer vorwärts drängend.
1. 2. Fl.
1. 2. Picc.
1. 2. Ob.
3. 4.
1. 2. 3. in B Clar.
1. 2. in Es
1. 2. Fag.
3.
Contrafag.
1. 2. Horn in F
3. 4. Horn in F
5. 6.
1. 2. Trmp. in F
3. 4. Trmp. in F
5. 6.
1. 2. Pos.
3. 4.
Tuba
1 Viol.
2. Viol.
Viola
Cello
Bass
zu 2.
zu 3.
gliss.
pizz.
arco
geth.
Immer vorwärts drängend.
Immer vorwärts drängend.

Mit einem Male etwas wuchtiger.
Pesante
289
1. 2. Fl.
1. 2. Picc.
1. 2. Ob.
1. 2. Fag.
3.
Contrafag.
1. 2. Horn in F.
3. 4. Horn in F.
5. 6.
1. 2. 5. Trmp. in F.
3. Trmp. in F.
4.
1. 2. Pos.
Becken
(mit Tellern)
2. Pauke
Mit einem Male etwas wuchtiger.
Pesante.
1. Viol.
geth.
2. Viol.
Viola
Cello
Bass
Pesante
Mit einem Male etwas wuchtiger.

294
19
1.2. Fl.
1.2. Ob.
3.4.
1.2.3. in B. Clar.
1.2. in Es.
1.2 Fag.
3.
Contrafag.
1.2. Horn in F.
3.4. Horn in F.
5.6.
1.2.5. Trmp. in F.
3. Trmp. in F.
4.
1.2. Pos.
3.4.
Tuba
Triangel
Becken
1. Pauke 2.
1.Viol.
2.Viol.
Viola
Cello
Bass
zu 2.
zu 3.
ohne Nachschl.
ff sempre
C nach B

172

176

395
26
Più mosso.
accel.
1.2. Fl.
1.2. Picc.
1. 2. Ob. 3. 4.
1.2.3. in B. Clar.
1.2. in Es.
1. 2. Fag. 3.
Contrafag.
1. 2. Horn in F.
3. 4. Horn in F.
5. 6.
1. 2. Trmp. in F.
3. 4. Trmp. in F.
5. 6.
1. 2. Pos. 3. 4.
Tuba.
Triangel.
Gr. Trom.
Becken.
Tam-tam. (tief.)
1. Pauke 2.
1. Viol.
2. Viol.
Viola.
Cello.
Bass.
zu 2
zu 3.
Zungenstoss
Zungenst.
mit aufgehobenem Schalltrichter
gestopft
offen
cresc.
sehr kurz
sempre cresc.
molto cresc.
sempre ff
mit Paukenschlägeln
klingen lassen
G nach Des

molto accelerando
Ganze Takte schlagen.
Poco rit.
405
1.2. Fl.
1.2. Picc
1.2. Ob. 3.4.
1.2.3. in B. Clar. 1.2. in Es.
1. Fag. 2. 3.
Contrafag.
1.2. Horn in F. 3.4. Horn in F. 5.6.
1.2. Trmp. in F. 3.4. Trmp. in F. 5.6.
1.2. Pos. 3.4.
Tuba
molto accelerando.
Triangel.
Gr. Trom.
Becken.
Tam-tam.
Pauke. 1. 2.
1 Viol.
2 Viol.
Viola.
Cello.
Bass.
sempre ff
Poco rit.
molto accelerando.
Ganze Takte schlagen.
Poco rit.
3. 4. 5. 6. Trompete und 1. Pauke nehmen ihren Platz „in weiter Ferne“ ein.

Anmerkung für den Dirigenten: die 4 Trompeten müssen aus entgegengesetzter Richtung her erklingen.

Zur Vereinfachung des orchestralen Apparates ist darauf Rücksicht genommen, dass diese Trompeten, falls es nöthig ist, von den im Orchester wirkenden Musikern (3.4.5.6. Trompete) ausgeführt werden können, und haben dieselben Zeit genug, ihre Plätze zu wechseln.

(Anmerkung: Die Striche | bedeuten die Stelle, wo die verschiedenen Instrumente im Rhythmus zusammenfallen sollen.)

*) Anmerkung für das Studium: Die 2. Bässe nicht eine Octave höher, sonst würde die vom Autor intendirte Wirkung ausbleiben; es kommt durchaus nicht darauf an, diese tiefen Töne zu hören, sondern durch diese Schreibart sollen nur die tiefen Bässe verhindert werden, etwa das obere B zu „nehmen" und so die obere Note zu verstärken.

Anmerkung für den Dirigenten: Die früher in der Ferne aufgestellten 4 Hörner mögen zur Verstärkung dieses Thema's herangezogen werden, ebenso in allen darauf folgenden eigens bezeichneten Stellen.

189

194

198

*) Anmerkung für den Dirigenten: Um die Continuität des Tempo's zu befestigen, empfiehlt es sich, in den ersten Takten noch Viertel anzuschlagen.

END OF EDITION

DOVER FULL-SIZE ORCHESTRAL SCORES

THE SIX BRANDENBURG CONCERTOS AND THE FOUR ORCHESTRAL SUITES IN FULL SCORE, Johann Sebastian Bach. Complete standard Bach-Gesellschaft editions in large, clear format. Study score. 273pp. 9 × 12.　　　　　　　　　　23376-6 Pa. **$11.95**

COMPLETE CONCERTI FOR SOLO KEYBOARD AND OR-CHESTRA IN FULL SCORE, Johann Sebastian Bach. Bach's seven complete concerti for solo keyboard and orchestra in full score from the authoritative Bach-Gesellschaft edition. 206pp. 9 × 12.
24929-8 Pa. **$11.95**

THE THREE VIOLIN CONCERTI IN FULL SCORE, Johann Sebastian Bach. Concerto in A Minor, BWV 1041; Concerto in E Major, BWV 1042; and Concerto for Two Violins in D Minor, BWV 1043. Bach-Gesellschaft edition. 64pp. 9⅜ × 12¼.　　　25124-1 Pa. **$6.95**

GREAT ORGAN CONCERTI, OPP. 4 & 7, IN FULL SCORE, George Frideric Handel. 12 organ concerti composed by great Baroque master are reproduced in full score from the *Deutsche Handelgesell-schaft* edition. 138pp. 9⅜ × 12¼.　　　　　　24462-8 Pa. **$8.95**

COMPLETE CONCERTI GROSSI IN FULL SCORE, George Frideric Handel. Monumental Opus 6 Concerti Grossi, Opus 3 and "Alexander's Feast" Concerti Grossi—19 in all—reproduced from most authoritative edition. 258pp. 9⅜ × 12¼.　　　　24187-4 Pa. **$13.95**

LATER SYMPHONIES, Wolfgang A. Mozart. Full orchestral scores to last symphonies (Nos. 35–41) reproduced from definitive Breitkopf & Härtel Complete Works edition. Study score. 285pp. 9 × 12.
23052-X Pa. **$12.95**

PIANO CONCERTOS NOS. 17–22, Wolfgang Amadeus Mozart. Six complete piano concertos in full score, with Mozart's own cadenzas for Nos. 17–19. Breitkopf & Härtel edition. Study score. 370pp. 9⅜ × 12¼.
23599-8 Pa. **$16.95**